J'APPRENDS
MES TOUT PREMIERS MOTS
ANGLAIS

Chantecler

Avant-propos

La première étape de l'apprentissage d'une langue étrangère est l'étude du vocabulaire. Lorsque tu connais le vocabulaire de base, tu peux ensuite apprendre l'orthographe, la grammaire, etc.

Tu trouveras dans ce livre les mots anglais les plus courants. Ils sont classés par thèmes; tu apprendras ainsi des mots simples sur la famille, la ferme, les animaux, et beaucoup d'autres. A côté de chaque illustration se trouve le mot anglais correspondant.

Si tu rencontres un mot anglais que tu ne comprends pas, tu peux le rechercher dans la liste placée en fin de page. A côté de chaque mot anglais est indiquée, en effet, sa traduction française.

A présent, au travail! Tu seras surpris de constater à quel point il est amusant de pouvoir jongler avec les mots en anglais.

Table des matières

The family

the sister

the brother

the father

the mother

to play football

The family

to draw

to run

to swim

Tu dois connaître ces mots:	
the family	la famille
the brother	le frère
the sister	la sœur
the father	le père
the mother	la mère
to play football	jouer au football
to draw	dessiner
to run	courir
to swim	nager

The classroom

the boy

the girl

the teacher

to write

to sing

The classroom

the pencil case

the book

the ballpoint

the scissors

the ruler

Tu dois connaître ces mots:	
the classroom	la classe
the boy	le garçon
the girl	la fille
the teacher	l'institutrice
to write	écrire
to sing	chanter
the book	le livre
the pencil case	le plumier
the ballpoint	le stylo à bille
the ruler	la règle
the scissors	les ciseaux

To count

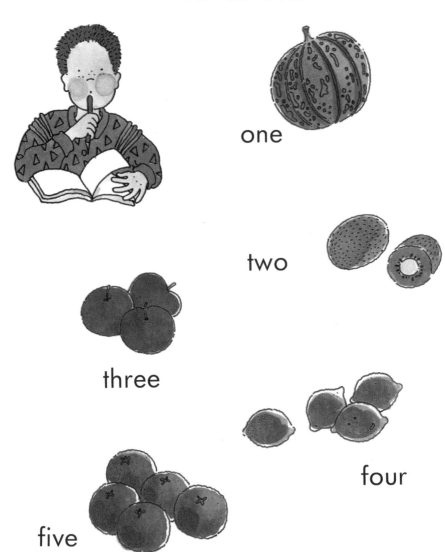

one

two

three

four

five

six

To count

seven

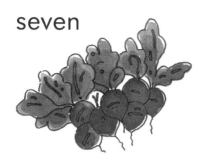

eight

nine

ten

The farm

the cock

the horse

the cow

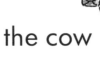

the sheep

the goat

The farm

the pig

the goose

the dog   the cat

the rabbit

Tu dois connaître ces mots:

the farm	la ferme
the cock	le coq
the horse	le cheval
the cow	la vache
the sheep	le mouton
the goat	la chèvre
the goose	l'oie
the dog	le chien
the cat	le chat
the rabbit	le lapin
the pig	le cochon

The animals

the monkey

the elephant

the lion

the crocodile

The animals

the giraffe

the bear

the kangaroo

Tu dois connaître ces mots:

the animals	les animaux
the monkey	le singe
the elephant	l'éléphant
the lion	le lion
the crocodile	le crocodile
the bear	l'ours
the giraffe	la girafe
the kangaroo	le kangourou

The weather

the snow

the freezing weather

the fog

the wind

The weather

the storm

the sun

the rain

Tu dois connaître ces mots:

the weather	le temps
the snow	la neige
the freezing weather	le gel
the fog	le brouillard
the wind	le vent
the storm	l'orage
the sun	le soleil
the rain	la pluie

Fruits and vegetables

the pineapple

the apple

the pear

the orange

the grape

Fruits and vegetables

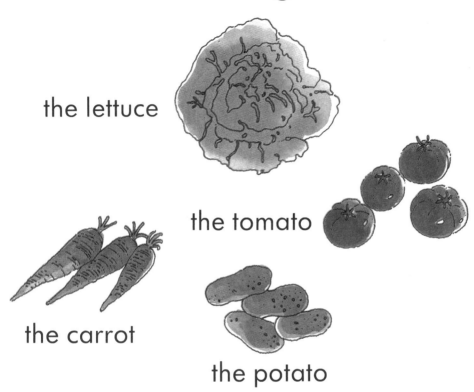

the lettuce

the tomato

the carrot

the potato

Tu dois connaître ces mots:

fruits and vegetables	les fruits et les légumes
the pineapple	l'ananas
the apple	la pomme
the pear	la poire
the orange	l'orange
the grape	le raisin
the lettuce	la salade
the tomato	la tomate
the carrot	la carotte
the potato	la pomme de terre

The methods of transport

the bicycle

the train

the lorry

the bus

the motorcycle

The methods of transport

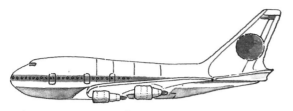

the aeroplane

the car

the ship

Tu dois connaître ces mots:

the methods of transport	les moyens de transport
the bicycle	la bicyclette
the train	le train
the lorry	le camion
the bus	l'autobus
the motorcycle	la moto
the aeroplane	l'avion
the car	la voiture
the ship	le bateau

The holiday

to skip

to play badminton

to play in the water

to fight

to do a jig-saw

The holiday

the sea

the parasol

the sandcastle

Tu dois connaître ces mots:	
the holiday	les vacances
to skip	sauter à la corde
to play badminton	jouer au badminton
to play in the water	jouer dans l'eau
to fight	se battre
to do a jig-saw	faire un puzzle
the sea	la mer
the parasol	le parasol
the sandcastle	le château de sable

23

To play

to shout

to whistle

to cry

to kiss

to get angry

To play

to laugh

to sweat

to sleep

Tu dois connaître ces mots:

to play	jouer
to shout	crier
to whistle	siffler
to cry	pleurer
to kiss	embrasser
to get angry	se fâcher
to laugh	rire
to sweat	transpirer
to sleep	dormir

The evening

to wash
one's hair

to brush
one's teeth

the bath

to dry
oneself

to do
one's hair

The evening

to put on
one's pyjama

to clean one's ears

to read

Tu dois connaître ces mots:

the evening	le soir
to brush one's teeth	se laver les dents
to wash one's hair	se laver les cheveux
the bath	le bain
to dry oneself	se sécher
to do one's hair	se coiffer
to put on one's pyjama	mettre son pyjama
to clean one's ears	nettoyer les oreilles
to read	lire

Word list

the family: la famille
the brother: le frère
the sister: la sœur
the father: le père
the mother: la mère
to play football: jouer au football
to draw: dessiner
to run: courir
to swim: nager

the classroom: la classe
the boy: le garçon
the girl: la fille
the teacher: l'institutrice
to write: écrire
to sing: chanter
the book: le livre
the pencil case: le plumier
the ballpoint: le stylo à bille
the ruler: la règle
the scissors: les ciseaux

to count: compter
one: un
two: deux
three: trois
four: quatre
five: cinq
six: six
seven: sept
eight: huit
nine: neuf
ten: dix

the farm: la ferme
the cock: le coq
the horse: le cheval
the cow: la vache
the sheep: le mouton
the goat: la chèvre
the goose: l'oie
the dog: le chien
the cat: le chat
the rabbit: le lapin
the pig: le cochon

the animals: les animaux
the monkey: le singe
the elephant: l'éléphant
the lion: le lion
the crocodile: le crocodile
the bear: l'ours
the giraffe: la girafe
the kangaroo: le kangourou

the weather: le temps
the snow: la neige
the freezing weather: le gel
the fog: le brouillard
the wind: le vent
the storm: l'orage
the sun: le soleil
the rain: la pluie

fruits and vegetables: les fruits et les
légumes
the pineapple: l'ananas
the apple: la pomme
the pear: la poire
the orange: l'orange
the grape: le raisin
the lettuce: la salade
the tomato: la tomate
the carrot: la carotte
the potato: la pomme de terre

the methods of transport: les moyens de
transport
the bicycle: la bicyclette
the train: le train
the lorry: le camion
the bus: l'autobus
the motorcycle: la moto
the aeroplane: l'avion
the car: la voiture
the ship: le bateau

Word list

the holiday: les vacances
to skip: sauter à la corde
to play badminton: jouer au badminton
to play in the water: jouer dans l'eau
to fight: se battre
to do a jig-saw: faire un puzzle
the sea: la mer
the parasol: le parasol
the sandcastle: le château de sable

to play: jouer
to shout: crier
to whistle: siffler
to cry: pleurer
to kiss: embrasser
to get angry: se fâcher
to laugh: rire
to sweat: transpirer
to sleep: dormir

the evening: le soir
to brush one's teeth: se laver les dents
to wash one's hair: se laver les cheveux
the bath: le bain
to dry oneself: se sécher
to do one's hair: se coiffer
to put on one's pyjama: mettre son
pyjama
to clean one's ears: nettoyer les oreilles
to read: lire